Kevin S. Gallagher, AIF

Is Your Financial Advisor

FAILING YOU?

AND HOW TO TELL

outskirts
press

TABLE OF CONTENTS

PREFACE

This book was written for the investor—*period*!

ONE THING YOU must understand prior to reading this book: Most "Financial Advisors," "Wealth Managers," "Money Managers," "Financial Planners"—whatever title they decide to use—came into the industry in one of two ways: 1. Either straight out of college with a degree in almost anything, or 2. As a result of a career change (mostly from some previous "sales job").

I, of course, am no different. I came into the financial industry three months after having graduated from college with a degree in Secondary Education. I was newly married, and my wife and I were living in the basement of my parents' home. We were completely broke and had no experience and no knowledge of any real-life money matters; yet, I was hired by a firm that aggressively pushed the latest *". . . You gotta get in now"* penny stocks to high net worth investors.

Think about it. There I was, not even paying my own bills yet, trying to sell highly speculative stocks to lifelong, successful people who were twenty, thirty, even forty or more years my senior. Looking back on it, I had absolutely no right being on the phone with those people, talking to them as if I had a clue about how one should manage and invest their own money.

The funny thing is, I did pretty well at it. "How?" you might ask. Simple: I was trained to be a "salesman." I was explicitly trained, tutored, and taught how to look, act, and sound "the part." I spoke with confidence and fooled them all . . . not to mention myself, in the process.

Looking back almost twenty-five years later, I think to myself ". . . how foolish I was." Even more so, I think about how foolish my clients were. Yet, the blame lies squarely on me—not the unsuspecting clients. What those clients saw was polish. What they heard was memorized. What they felt was confidence. But what they got was a sales job!

Fortunately, for me and my current clients, my first experience in the investment industry is in my past. However, for most investors reading this book, that polished, refined, and well-spoken salesman who I was then is most likely the exact same kind of character that they are taking financial advice from today!

The good news, however, is that I have written this book with only the investor in mind. My colleagues in the financial services industry are most certainly not going to like this book. In fact, as much as we in the investment world do not like to use the word "guarantee," there is one guarantee I am comfortable making: If you have a financial advisor who is nothing more than a polished salesperson, he or she will

> **If you have a financial advisor who is nothing more than a polished salesperson, he or she will most likely try like heck to discredit this book.**

most likely try like heck to discredit this book. If, however, you are working with and taking advice from a competent advisor who has only your best interest at heart, he or she will likely applaud this book.

Over the two decades or so since my initial "stock pushing" salesman experience, I have gone on to a series of experiences and successes that have moved me away from selling and more toward a knowledge of how investing really works. I spent a couple of years at one of the industry's most respected socially conscience mutual fund companies where I was exposed to some wonderful portfolio managers who taught me that risk management often leads to greater long-term success than does the blind desire for chasing returns. I then went to work for one of Wall Street's most highly respected and well-known wire house firms.

But the biggest, most powerful experience that shaped my knowledge of how investing truly works was when I was invited to be a member of the Philadelphia Stock Exchange (yes, there really is a stock exchange in Philadelphia). I became a professional floor trader. I found myself at the epicenter of our financial system, trading my own account as a sophisticated, derivatives market maker in what was at that time the largest, most actively traded sector index in the world. Portfolio management theory began to play an increasingly important part in my life. I read countless numbers of books on trading, asset management theory, and risk mitigation strategies. At that time, my livelihood directly depended on my ability to create and manage well diversified, risk-appropriate portfolios that not only gave me a good shot at making money but most importantly, kept me from losing large chunks of money in the event that the markets went against me (and they often did).

Now—and many years after having enjoyed a rather successful experience as a professional, multimillion-dollar trader—my career path has seemingly come full-circle. After leaving the exchange floor, I took a few years off from the "real world" and simply enjoyed life and the fruits of my trading career. I, of course, continued to trade and invest my own money to support my family. Over dinner one evening, though, a dear friend of mine asked, *"So, what are you going to do now?"* The answer—truthfully at that time was—*"I don't really know yet."* She then mentioned that she had a business client who owned a medium-sized, independent financial planning firm and that he was looking to expand and grow his business. I said, *"No, thanks."* Going back into the "sales world" was not for me. She then said one more thing. She said, *". . . didn't you originally go to college to be a teacher? Because this guy's firm specializes in working with educators in the local area and helping them put together their retirement plans."* Having gone to school to be a teacher, I was, to say the least, intrigued.

However, intrigue quickly gave way to the realities of the financial services industry. As I transitioned back into the "retail" side of the investment industry—armed with a deep appreciation and knowledge of how to create well diversified, risk-appropriate portfolios—what I was finding was that prospective clients would come to me to review their investments . . . and their portfolios were a disaster. In case after case, I would meet families who would come to me with a portfolio of investments, selected by a supposedly well-educated financial advisor, who—more often than not—would have nothing even remotely close to a well diversified, risk-appropriate portfolio based on any kind of respected, sound investment theory. What I sadly learned—almost twenty years after my first experience as a stock pusher—is that the financial "salesman" is still alive and well. And, in fact, is probably craftier and more polished than ever before.

If I could reduce the message within these pages to one sentence, it would be: "Do not confuse a *wealthy* financial advisor with a *competent* financial advisor." Most wealthy, successful financial advisors got that way not necessarily because they know more about investing than do their clients, but because they know more about "selling" investments to their clients. They pushed their opinions and marketing materials on unsuspecting prospects and clients. They created their wealth by charging commissions and fees in a variety of ways not so easily detected. There are very few (rare, in fact) wealthy financial advisors who became that way by investing their own money. And doesn't it stand to reason that it probably makes more sense to have your money managed by a great *investor* rather than a great *salesperson* in a well tailored suit?

The pages that follow are intended to open your eyes, to expose the reality and truths behind the suggestions and opinions of the overwhelming majority of those people we call "financial professionals." The fact is, most financial firms—especially the big ones—couldn't care less about the financial skills of their advisors. They do, however, care about and spend significant time and resources developing their sales skills. Most successful financial advisors are successful sales-men. You probably have one.

As you read the pages that follow, you will begin to understand better who is managing your money—a true, valuable "Financial Advisor," or the all too common "Financial Salesman."

CHAPTER

FINANCIAL ADVISOR
OR SALESMAN

LIKE MOST PEOPLE, during the first few years of my career, I bounced around from firm to firm and position to position within my chosen industry. However, I always kept my eye on what I believed to be my ultimate goal: a position as a "Financial Consultant" with one of Wall Street's most prestigious firms. I felt that if I could get to that level, I'd be introduced and exposed to people far smarter than I, who would then open their private vault of sophisticated money secrets to me. I would then take this new knowledge and demonstrate to my future clients just how smart I was. This, of course, would lead to a glorious career abounding with advancement and significant compensation. Ah, the fallacies of youth!

Three and a half years after my first job of pushing penny stocks, I finally achieved my goal (well, at least *part* of it). At the age of twenty-six, newly married, and generally knowing not a thing about investments and financial strategies, I was hired as a financial consultant in the Washington, D.C., office of one of the world's most well-known and dominant Wall Street firms.

Specifically, I was hired to prospect and develop the all-important "high net worth," private client market. The good news for me was that a newly titled financial consultant could hardly find himself in a better geographic area than the Washington, D.C., metropolitan region. If I was being asked to find wealthy people, I was in the right place. In fact, year after year, the Washington, D.C., metro area and its surrounding counties are almost always ranked among the wealthiest areas in the nation. Furthermore, unlike other pockets of wealth scattered all across the United States, I found myself working in an area that was not only densely populated with such wealth, but far greater in terms of geographic square miles than any other place I had ever lived. The wealth factor of this region was (and still is) massive—and I was about to tell them all how smart money management was actually done!

So, as massive as the potential pool of prospects was, and as lucky as I felt, there was one thing that I failed to realize. As it turns out, I was not the only person on the planet, nor was my new employer the only firm in the area, that realized, appreciated, and very much wanted to capitalize on exploiting the sizable market of wealthy individuals living in and around the D.C. area. The reality was that from every major Wall Street firm, all the way down to the mom-and-pop financial planning offices, and everyone in between, there existed tremendous competition for the same clients. So, while still being excited about my potential to tap into this market, I was becoming increasingly aware of the size, skill, and determination of my competition.

My problems were no different than any other company's challenges when they find themselves in a highly profitable, highly competitive market—regardless of the product or service. Simply put, the only way any company can compete in competitive environments is to have legions of highly trained, highly motivated salespeople—and the financial services industry is no exception to that rule. In fact, it only took a few days in my new dream job before the branch manager walked in to greet the new recruits with a speech designed squarely to define our new roles within the firm.

Looking back, I can say that I was the perfect blend of ignorance, motivation, and stupidity. I was also about to add to the mix "jaded."

You see, I had it stuck in my mind that if I made it to a top-tier firm, they would teach me how to be a top-tier financial advisor. I assumed that my new colleagues, who had been practicing their crafts for decades, were now going to bestow upon me the secrets of sophisticated financial know-how. I would then be armed and ready to go out into the world to advise the wealthy on how to become even *wealthier*. I could not wait to know all that I did not yet know. Fortunately for me, I did not have to wait long.

> **The reality was that from every major Wall Street firm, all the way down to the mom-and-pop financial planning offices, and every one in between, there existed tremendous competition for the same clients.**

On one of the first Fridays on the job, the branch manager called an early-morning meeting of all the newly hired financial consultants. This man was, to say the least, a larger-than-life personality. He was literally a legend within the industry—a near godlike figure within the walls of our office. I remember walking into the conference room thinking how fortunate I was to be in a position to hear from one of our industry's smartest representatives; one of the most well-known and respected financial consultants of our times. I could hardly wait to hear what words of wisdom this giant of our industry was about to dispense.

And so . . . The giant spoke. His words were short and simple, yet very direct and clear. He told us exactly what we would need to know to be successful financial consultants. Although I can no longer quote him directly, I can certainly paraphrase his mind-blowing advice. He said, *". . . do not make the mistake of believing that you are financial advisors. It is nothing more than a title we use for the public. What you are—in reality—are 'Salesmen and -Women.' Nothing more, and nothing less. You just happen to sell financial services and packaged financial products. Be proud of it. Learn to be great salespeople. And learn to make a lot of money . . ."* And although the giant continued to speak, it has been too many years to recall the entirety of his words. However, his basic pitch to us was that we were on par with all other salespeople in the world—don't let the fancy ties and sharp suits fool us (do, however, let them fool your clients).

The giant did, however, end on a high note. In an attempt to motivate his new crop of financial consultant salespeople, he threw out a challenge. In order to generate competitive desires among his freshman class of salesmen, he identified two members that he believed would be the ones for the rest of us to beat. He said that they had all the markings and talents necessary to be the best in our class. Of these two future stars, one was a former car salesman, and the other, a former office supply sales representative. I had expected the bar to be set a bit higher.

Coming out of that meeting, I remember thinking to myself, *"What?! Am I in the right place? Am I working for the firm I thought I was? Were those really the words of one of the most respected, most successful financial advisors in our industry? Is this really what it's all about?"* The answers, of course, were: yes, yes, and yes! The reality that began to sink in was that I was ignorant and misled by my own perceptions and assumptions of what it means to be a financial advisor. My guess is that as an investor who is reading this book, you have been equally misled—and you're about to learn how.

Here now is why this story is important to the average investor who seeks what they believe to be sophisticated advice from the average financial advisor. When I entered one of Wall Street's top firms as a new employee, I was not much different in my expectations and perceptions of that firm—or others like it—than most investors are when they too walk into firms like that. I assumed, as I believe the vast majority of investors assume, that a

> **The hard truth is that the overwhelming majority of financial advisors, regardless of who they work for, are nothing more than glorified, overpaid, well-groomed salesmen—period.**

financial advisor is an individual who knows, recommends, and applies incredibly sophisticated financial strategies to fulfill their client's needs. I have now learned that like almost every investor, I was wrong. The hard truth is that the overwhelming majority of financial advisors—regardless of who they work for—are nothing more than glorified, overpaid, well-groomed salesmen—period.

The good news here is that these so-called financial advisors only represent the "vast majority." Which means, by definition, that there must be a few really good, true financial advisors out there whose advice and guidance really do matter. The question then is: *"How do you tell one from the other?"*

The answer to such a question is not always so easy. In fact, not even I could distinguish the wolf from the sheep until I had accumulated a wealth of experience as a professional trader and portfolio manager. You see, unless you have significant knowledge and understanding about how the investment industry really works, and unless you have an appreciation for sound investment strategy, you will almost certainly fall victim to the marketing and sales approach of the ubiquitous financial sales rep.

What follows in the pages of this book are what I believe to be the most pervasive and easy to identify markers and red flags that your financial advisor is potentially nothing more than a salesperson. Since it is my belief—and my experience—that the majority of my industry colleagues are of the "sales rep" ilk, I believe that most readers will, unfortunately, find that their trusted advisor fits squarely into more than one of the following categories. Prepare to be awakened.

CHAPTER **II**

IT'S ALL IN THE (SAME) FAMILY

LOOKING BACK OVER my childhood, I can fondly recall some of my most cherished memories are of summer vacations at the beach. There was always something to do, from going to the boardwalk, playing in the arcades, riding roller coasters at the amusement park, to just hanging out on the sand with my five brothers—nothing like it. Among those memories was when I would watch the lifeguards doing their jobs.

Before the age of cell phones and text messaging, if the beach patrol lifeguards needed to communicate with one another all the way up and down the length of the beach, they would resort to what seemed to me a complex, secret, choreographed use of waving red flags. As a young boy of six years of age, I can remember being mes- merized as one guard would stand tall in his chair and begin waving his red flags around in some mysterious pattern that evidently meant something to another lifeguard three blocks to the north. The flags— as you can imagine—were bright red, a color most likely chosen for two reasons: First, they were easy to see. Second, the system was meant to warn of pending danger.

Well, much like those beach patrols of my youth, I write this chapter with two hypothetical red flags waving at you. Although you are not likely to actually see any red flags on these pages, you will be made aware of possible dangers.

One of the simplest ways to know whether you are working with a truly talented financial advisor or just a "salesman-in-sheep's-clothing" is, quite simply, to look at the recommended investments in your portfolio. If you have been advised to invest in multiple mutual funds for the sake of diversification but notice on your statements that they are all from the same fund company (or sometimes known as a "fund family"), there is a better than even chance that you are dealing with someone who is nothing more than a salesman who happens to work in the financial services industry.

Let me be clear: In all my years as a professional trader and now as a comprehensive financial advisor and asset manager, I have yet to see any valid research that suggests a qualitative advantage to having all of a client's investable assets with one fund company. In fact, to the contrary, there exists a significant, credible rationale that strongly suggests that one should never place all of their money with the same fund family. This then begs the question: Why do so many supposed, intelligent financial advisors place so many clients' assets all in the same fund family? The answer is often threefold: ease of operations, ignorance, and compensation.

First, the overwhelming majority of financial salespeople place all of their clients' money into just one fund company because it's easy—period! To borrow a line from the office supply company Staples, it's the "Easy Button." Think about it . . . How much work, time, effort, understanding, intelligence,

> . . . waving at you like a big, red flag!

criteria, and analysis must it take for someone to recommend that you just sink all of your hard-earned money into one fund company? The answer, of course, is "none." Heck, you can do that yourself (and without paying anyone). Yet, most clients originally seek out the advice of financial advisors because they assume that the advisor—or his or her firm—has some knowledge of how to invest that is far more sophisticated than that which the client can come up with on his or her own. Clients of financial salespeople often believe wholeheart-edly that their advisor is applying some complex set of criteria to help determine which of the tens of thousands of available invest-ment choices are the best to include in the client's portfolio. Yet, in reality, nothing can be further from the truth, and the evidence is right there on the client's quarterly statements—waving at you like a big, red flag!

If you notice that your account with your trusted financial advisor is made up exclusively (or mostly) of funds all coming from the same company, then it's safe to say that your advisor is most likely doing nothing for you. He or she is failing you, and you are paying them for it. The brutal truth is that within the financial services industry, there exists no shortage of financial professionals who are incredibly competent at only one thing: selling people on the idea of opening a new account. The client, naturally, actually believes that after they opened the account that the advisor is back at his office monitoring and analyzing the portfolio daily. Yet, in most cases, this is not even close to what really happens after an account is opened. In most cases, the advisor moves on to open accounts with other unsuspect-ing prospects; and, there is almost no way that the client could know any different.

Clients are often convinced that their financial advisor is doing a wonderful job. They look at their statements and see funds with lots of different names. This, typically, is interpreted by the client as them being well diversified. And we've all heard that it's a good idea to be diversified, right? Diversification is, of course, a great idea. Generally speaking, the reason for diversification is to reduce the overall inherent risk associated with investing, by spreading your money across lots of different segments of the economy that may or may not react similarly in response to adverse market and economic conditions. Any rookie financial advisor should understand and apply basic diversification strategies with their clients. After all, who doesn't remember the age-old adage: *"Never put all of your eggs in one basket"*? Diversification just makes sense on many levels. So then, when clients notice that their financial advisor has spread their money into a number of different mutual funds, the client confidently assumes that they are dealing with a competent professional.

Well, not so fast. While I will certainly applaud any advisor who understands and recommends well thought out diversification strategies, I will quickly condemn them if they simply hit the "Easy Button" by filling in each investment category with mutual funds all from the same fund family. To do this is a rookie mistake of incompetence—regardless of how many years the advisor has been in the business.

There are some compelling reasons why one ought not to be invested all in the same fund company. First, while it may be true that a certain fund company is well regarded, the problem is that investors—and financial advisors—confuse the "company" with the "products." For example, I live in the state of Maryland. In my state resides one of the industry's largest, most well-known mutual fund families. They represent—for lack of a better explanation—a great Maryland, homegrown, success story. That success story, however, is more associated with the success of the company—not necessarily with the quality of its individual mutual funds. This is an important distinction because most of us are not investing in the "company"; we're investing in its "products." The products of a mutual fund company are, naturally, mutual funds. And each individual mutual fund is typically run as a separate business entity of the mutual fund company. Herein lies the problem: As with any complex, multilevel, multiproduct-line company, it is impossible for them to do all things perfectly and at the highest level.

Mutual fund companies consisting sometimes of dozens or more funds are no different than any other company in any other business—a

> **Mutual fund companies consisting sometimes of dozens or more funds, are no different then any other company in any other business—a few of their products are worth having—but the vast majority are not.**

few of their products are worth having—but the vast majority are not. In fact, in my experience, it is rare to find a mutual fund company with more than just a few of their funds performing at the highest levels when compared to all other funds. Even more alarming is that most fund companies don't even have a *single* fund that would be considered the best in its class.

Said another way, the majority of mutual funds available to investors throughout the entire investment industry are laggards and poor performers relative to their competitors. That being the case, if it is recommended that you put a large portion of your investment dollars into multiple funds from a single mutual fund company, you have unknowingly been sold an investment portfolio that is very likely made up of very poor-performing investments.

Another strong argument against placing all of an investor's money in one fund company is that much of the research being used by all of the different mutual fund managers within a single mutual fund company is produced by a single research department within that mutual fund company. Fund companies spend considerable amounts of money and manpower developing complex research departments. For those fund companies that do not develop their own research departments, they still spend inordinate sums of money contracting with independent, third-party, research analysts. Either way, fund companies spend millions on market research and are often getting the majority of it from one source. This creates implied pressure on the fund managers to use the research being provided by his or her employer.

As a result, it is a fair statement to say that a fund company's aggregate performance across all their individual funds is extremely reliant on the research department providing data to the managers. If the research department is a good one, manned by competent staff analysis, then fund performance is likely to be relatively strong across all funds. This is, normally, in theory only. You see, there still are too many moving parts. As with any job, a research department's staff will come and go via employee turnover. Department heads move on to other departments or even entirely new firms. And then, there is the issue of the fund manager or managers (as many funds are now managed "by committee"). And what if the research is sound, but the manager is not? And what about the managers who like to have their own research source that may or may not conflict with the data being provided by the fund family at great expense? The bottom line is this: If the research being provided is of poor quality, it is likely that fund performance across all funds within a fund company is going to suffer. If your trusted advisor has placed you in funds of a single fund company, you may technically be diversified, but you have significantly increased the odds of poorer, relative performance over time.

Now, let's move to a more disturbing fact of my industry. If it's pretty much common sense that having all of your money invested in one fund company is a less-than-ideal situation, then why do so many financial advisors still place a large majority of their clients' assets with one fund company? Well, if not for it being the "easiest" path, then definitely for the following reason: Just follow the money trail right back to the advisor's pocket.

As I sit with new client after new client coming from other financial services firms and from a host of other financial advisors, I consistently see the same two or three fund companies in most people's portfolios. One must ask: In an industry of thousands of funds, how is it possible that the same few fund companies keep showing up in investor accounts—regardless of who their financial advisor is or what firm they work for? It's a great question. One for which I happen to have an answer.

It is almost always because these couple of fund companies are compensating financial advisors through what are known as the fund's "internal operating expenses" (or "internal fees"). Some of these fees, which are indeed shown and itemized in the mutual fund's prospectus, are nothing short of annual "kickbacks" to the advisor. It's an annual *"Thank you for sending your client's money to us."* And, wouldn't you know it . . . The very few funds that I see in almost all investors' accounts are from the fund companies with the highest internal fund expenses. Now, do you *really* believe that these funds are being sold by trusted financial advisors based on the fund's performance? Of course not. To be clear, most advisors today have the luxury and ability to choose investments and make client recommendations from a wide variety of sources and fund companies. However, all too often, they only recommend those funds which carry the highest internal fees. I wonder why . . .

Do you see any red flags yet? If not, do a simple review of one of your account statements. If you find that the majority of your investments are all from the same fund company, then I can tell you with almost complete conviction that your trusted advisor is either incompetent, hitting the "Easy Button," or just cashing in on your ignorance by putting you into high-expense funds which pay the advisor a nice annual incentive for recommending their funds. Either way, your performance over time is not likely to be as good as it could be.

The alternative is that portfolio creation by a trusted, worthy financial advisor can often be easily seen by the use of multiple different mutual funds from many different mutual fund companies. If the advisor really is independent in their thinking and approach, and they truly apply a sophisticated process by which they identify investments of excellence for inclusion in their clients' portfolios, and if they are really doing more for you than you can do for yourself, then the portfolios they create will very likely show selections from multiple different mutual fund companies. A well thought out, well designed, risk-appropriate portfolio will almost always be clearly identifiable by its use of different investment companies across different asset classes as the advisor's goal is to find fund companies that have particular expertise within the asset class the advisor is selecting. Asset classes that aren't of a fund company's expertise will almost always be filled by investment selections from different fund companies.

If a simple review of your accounts shows that your advisor (or maybe even you) has loaded your portfolio with investments and mutual funds from a single source, it might be time to consider finding a different professional to work with (or maybe to realize that you shouldn't be managing your own accounts).

CHAPTER

THE CLASS WARS:
A, B and C Shares

HERE'S AN INTERESTING wrinkle in the investment management industry that seemingly was created with the investor's best interest in mind (and when used properly and for very specific and strategic reasons, this wrinkle *can potentially be* in the best interest of *some* investors). That being said, when looked at critically, we can often see the "telltale signs" that differentiate the true financial advisor from the all-too-common financial salesman.

The "wrinkle" at hand is the different fee structures put in place by fund families in order to offer a variety of ways to purchase their products depending on the client's needs. Typically, this does not apply to traditional "no-load" funds that investors can purchase directly. However, most investment advisors don't recommend true "no-load" choices (unless you find an advisor who only recommends low-cost, no-load, institutional-class funds—which is typically a sign of an advisor who really is working with the client's best interests at heart). Instead, they typically offer "loaded" funds that offer a dizzying array of fee structures for the clients to choose from.

Now, before we launch into this topic, let me just set the record straight from the get-go: I am an absolutely committed believer that most investors should find and work with a professional financial advisor who actively guides and monitors their accounts. In fact, the entire purpose of this book is to help the average investor identify a competent advisor worth following and paying, while becoming alert to those who are just sales imposters. Once a good advisor is found, they're worth every penny. What's interesting is that most people who hire outstanding financial advisors and understand the value the advisor provides have very little concern with what they pay for the services. Many happy, well taken care of clients have no problem at all with paying fees—even relatively high fees to some advisors—provided they have concrete evidence of the value they are receiving for the expenses being paid. The problem is that in most cases, clients pay fees and receive in return not much more than what they could do for themselves for free. Wouldn't you agree that when someone declares that they are paying "too much in fees," what they really are saying is that they don't see what they're *getting* for what they are *paying*? Isn't it true that no matter what the type of service in question (car repairs, internet service provider, cell phone provider, etc.), we gladly pay the fee if we see the value? And, alternatively, we are disgusted by the fee if we think we get nothing for it? With that in mind, let's take a look at the traditional fee structures that many advisors apply when recommending mutual funds to their clients. More importantly, let's see if these fee structures can provide any insight into whether the advisor is really doing anything for the client, or if he/she is just a salesperson.

First, a simplified history lesson with respect to the evolution of fee structures within the mutual fund industry: Originally, there was mainly one way to buy a mutual fund. You typically called a broker—or in some cases, you would call the fund company directly—and you'd tell them which fund you wanted to

> **Isn't it true that no matter what the type of service in question . . . we gladly pay the fee if we see the value?**

own, how much of it you wanted to invest, and then sent a check for the amount. However, when you sent the check, you also had to cover the sales charge or commission (often called a "load"). This type of fee structure is commonly known as a "front-end load."

Currently, front-end loads can be as high as 5¾ percent of the initial amount invested for some of the industry's most often advisor-recommended funds. This is significant since the 5¾ percent comes out of the client's investment amount. Said in a different and more meaningful way, this represents a 5¾ percent *loss* to the client. As such, the client now needs the investment to have a return better than 5¾ percent, just to break even from the sales charge!

Today, this front-end load structure is often referred to as purchasing an "A" share class of a mutual fund. If an investor—either on his or her own or through an advisor—purchases an "A" share class of a mutual fund, he or she is likely going to pay the prevailing front-end load charged by that specific fund company.

But as we come forward in time during our fee structure history lesson, another fee structure began to take shape: The "B" share. This—as you can imagine—is just a "hybrid" of the "A" share. In fact, all that really was done was to hide the fees in a creative way. It allows the investor the ability to purchase the exact same fund as the "A" share but with a different fee structure. The first thing that the investor will notice between the "A" and "B" shares is that the "B" has a significantly lower front-end sales charge. In fact, "B" shares typically have half the front-end load charge of the "A" share. This would appear to be a better deal for the investor, right? After all, lower fees are always a good thing . . . aren't they? Well, not so fast . . .

Before being seduced by the lower front-end sales charge of the "B" share versus the "A" share, you must be made aware of some of the other unique differences between "A" shares and "B"s. In fact, once you understand the added characteristics of the "B" share, you will likely understand that all that the mutual fund industry really did was not much more than a "shell game." They simply moved the fees around in a nifty and creative way as to not really be noticed by the investor.

Here's how: The fund company, in an effort to offset the significant reduction in the front-end load, actually adds what is known as a "Contingent Deferred Sales Charge" (or CDSC). This is a charge for anyone who buys a "B" share and then sells it within a certain time—usually within seven years. That's right; they reduce the front-end sales charge just to move it to a "back-end" sales charge. Moreover, these "back-end" sales charges can often be as high as 3 percent.

Now, recall, a typical "A" share has a front-end sales charge of 5¾ percent. The "B" share has an industry average of about 2½ percent. Sounds pretty good . . . right? Well, not so much once you realize that the "back-end" sales charge they've added to it can be as high as 3 percent. Put the front-end charge of 2½ percent with the 3 percent CDSC, and, guess what? You're right back to about the total of the typical "A" share class. In essence, the fund company didn't reduce your fees at all. They just moved them around like an old-fashioned "shell game." Pretty nice of them, isn't it?

Now, if that's not enough, when the fund company decided to do the investor a favor by reducing the front-end load just so they could attach a back-end load, they also added another gem to the mix: far higher internal expenses! You see, all funds understandably have some internal expenses (even index funds typically have some cost associated with them). After all, there are actual, real people who have real jobs working at the fund company. They deserve to make a living just like the rest of us who go to work each day. Typically, the in-

> In essence, the fund company didn't reduce your fees at all. They just moved them around like an old-fashioned "shell game."

ternal expenses of an "A" share fund may range between 0.25 percent and 0.75 percent of the fund's total assets per year. But with the "B" share, the fund company often increases the internal expenses by almost double! Ironically, what this means is that "mathematically," it can actually be *less expensive* over time to own the "A" share with the higher up-front load and relatively lower internal expense than to own the "B" share with the more attractive, lower up-front charge but higher internal expense. This is because the longer an investor owns the "B" share, the longer that higher internal expense is chipping away at their returns. Interesting math, isn't it?

Here's another significant problem with owning a "B" share: They are virtually "proof positive" that the advisor who recommended it to you is nothing more than a salesperson. This is because financial advisors who recommend a share class that has a back-end sales charge which lasts nearly seven years is telling you beyond the shadow of a doubt that they are not intending in any way to manage your money. They are literally going to put your money into a fund and never move it based on any performance or criteria. If the fund performs poorly, you're stuck with it. Why? Well, think about it: If I were your financial advisor, and I recommended a "B" share that in two years started to be one of the worst-performing funds in its class, how would you respond if I called you and said something like, *"Hey, you know that fund I put you in and charged you 2½ percent to purchase? Well, it's a horrible performer now, and you've been doing very poorly in it. I'd like to suggest we get out of it and replace that investment with something else."*

If you were to get that phone call from me, you'd probably be pretty pleased at first. You would think that I was doing a fine job at watching over your nest egg and that I'm looking out for your best interest . . . until I ended my call with the following: *"Now, to get you out of the fund that I recommended and that is performing poorly, I'm going to charge you another 3 percent because it has a Contingent Deferred Sales Charge. Then, the next fund I'm going to put you in is going to be a 'B' share with some other fund company, and that's going to cost you another 2½ percent to get in. Sound good?"*

Of course not! You relied on me to find better investment choices than what you thought you could find on your own, and lo and behold, it turns out that the one I recommended is terrible. Now, I'm going to charge you to get out if it! Doesn't seem like a very good deal now, does it? But here's the good news: That phone call is NEVER going to happen! Why? Because if I'm the type of advisor who puts clients into "B" share funds, I am certainly not the type who's watching over the quality of their investments. Think about it: There is NO WAY that an advisor who sells "B" shares is going to call a client and tell them that their recommended fund is terrible and that the client isn't doing very well, so now, it's time to take a sales loss to get out of it.

The bottom line is that if you think an advisor is managing your money and looking out for you when things don't go as planned, I'm writing this chapter to tell you that if you have been recommended "B" share funds, the reality is that you are wrong. The advisor is clearly telling you by the very products they sell that he or she has absolutely *no intention* of ever moving your money—poor performance or not.

But just before you thought it couldn't get any sneakier, they came up with yet another evolution of the share class sales game: the "C" share. It works similarly to the "B" share in that it is a reduced front-end sales charge versus its "A" share counterpart. In fact, the "C" share tends to look extremely attractive to many investors and is a favorite of many financial salespeople. Here's why: The "C" share reduces the front-end sales charge all the way down to only 1 percent. That's a significant reduction from the "A" share and the "B." The "C" share, naturally, has a Contingent Deferred Sales Charge added to it, but with only about a one-year period. So far, so good, right?

Not so fast. This is just a "shell game" as well. The fees and charges aren't really as good as they look. In fact, they might even be worse over time. Remember those internal expenses and how the fund company increased them with the "B" share? Well, what do you think they've done with the "C" shares? You guessed it; they've increased them *even more* this time. It is not uncommon to find "C" share funds with internal expenses in the area of 2 percent of the fund's assets per year. That's a big expense that just keeps reducing your returns year after year.

If you're thinking, *"Well, wait a minute. If the 'C' share only has a one-year CDSC, then my advisor may certainly be the type that will call me if the fund starts to perform poorly since after only one year, I can sell the fund without penalty."* What's the problem with that? The answer is found if you just follow the money. You see, that higher, sometime much, *much* higher, internal expense associated with the "C" share doesn't just go to the fund company. A very large portion of it goes directly back to the financial salesperson who put you in the investment. This becomes an annual source of recurring revenue for the financial salesperson—a source of revenue that he or she is very unlikely to want to get rid of. As such, I'm just warning you: If you look through your investment account statements and find the letters "B" or "C" after the names of the funds you've purchased based on your advisor's recommendations, there is a very real chance that your advisor is doing nothing for you. Which, of course, begs the question: *"What the heck are you still paying them for . . . ?"*

So, what's an investor who's looking for advice to do? Well, the answer to that question is found throughout the pages of this book and will be covered more directly in the following chapters. But a good start is to stay away from advisors who recommend "B" and "C" share funds. Moreover, it is probably in your best interest to find an advisor who is "fee-based." These are advisors who charge their clients an annual "fee" typically based on a percentage of the client's assets that they manage. They typically DO NOT use commission-able funds with front-end or back-end sales charges or CDSCs. And, in most cases, they are far more likely to actually be in the business of "managing" their client's money and more likely to move things around if the performance is not what is desired. Why? Because they have no restrictions for moving in and out of funds for whatever rea-son! And, to do so adds no additional costs to the client. The fee-based advisor is typically the type of professional who WILL call a client and suggest that they move out of one fund and into another. With no Contingent Deferred Sales Charge time frames, there's no obstacle to getting rid of poor-performing funds and replacing them with higher-performing funds. This, of course, is what most investors "believe" a financial advisor is supposed to be doing for them. This approach often leads to better returns over time. Sadly, however, it is *not* the norm.

CHAPTER IV

STUCK IN THE BOX— TARGET DATE FUNDS

WITHIN THE LAST decade, so-called Target Date mutual funds have become one of the investment industry's hottest packaged products. Initially promoted by "no-load" fund companies, these investment products have now been adopted by almost every fund company in the industry—and for good reason: The simplicity associated with these investment vehicles make them a "can't miss" sales pitch. As a result, you are probably already familiar with these products and may even be invested in them; especially if your employer provides you a 401(k) or other employer-based retirement plan, where these products have become the absolute norm.

Here's a basic explanation on what they are and how they work: A Target Date mutual fund is one which is designed to reduce its overall market risk and stock market exposure over time, as the investor moves closer and closer to the "target date" that he or she is retiring or needs the money. Okay, that's what it is; now, here's how it's supposed to work. Let's say that you contact a financial advisor or go directly to a mutual fund company. You tell them that you are interested in saving

> **Within the last decade, so-called Target Date mutual funds have become one of the investment industry's hottest packaged products.**

for a specific life event—like retirement or college expenses for your child. Any financial advisor who has been in the business for at least one day will most likely ask, *"How many years until the event?"* Let's say your answer is thirteen years from now. Armed with that data, the wise advisor then says to you, *"Boy, oh boy, do we have the right thing for you . . ."* And what they suggest as the perfect fit for you is a Target Date Fund with a year attached to it that is thirteen years from now.

The explanation the advisor gives for why the product is perfect for you goes a little something like this: With a Target Date Fund, the investor contributes money to a professionally designed portfolio that automatically selects an investment mix from a menu of twenty or so mutual funds, all from the same fund company (first "red flag"). The selected mix of funds chosen becomes the "basket" of funds which make up the single Target Date Fund. Each individual fund within the basket is allocated a specific percentage of the investor's money. Sounds pretty smart so far, doesn't it? Well, it gets even better.

Not only do these Target Date Funds automatically determine how much of the investor's money should go to each of the individual funds, but on some regular basis (usually once per year), the same professionally managed portfolio will "rebalance" the amount to each fund in an effort to reduce risk as the investor nears the event for which they are saving. It couldn't get any better, right?

This, of course, make complete logical sense. Most investors would readily agree that they would not want to expose their savings to too much market risk as they approach their desired retirement date for fear of potentially losing their money just before they actually need it. And since rebalancing does indeed help to reduce risk, the investor need not worry about a thing. They can just send their money in, sit back, and relax until retirement day. Wow! Who knew it could be so good?

Well, not so fast . . .

I would agree that the logic behind these investment vehicles sounds great. In fact, I would have to say I love the concept. Think about it: The investor identifies when they need access to their money, and then they just start contributing to the account. There's nothing else to do. From the investor's point of view (and this actually becomes much of the sales pitch), it can't get any easier. Again, it's a great concept—I just question the actual implementation of the strategy. I believe you should, as well.

Let's take a closer look at what's really going on in these products. Let's explore why these products were really created in the first place. Because in my humble opinion, I don't think they were initially created with the investor in mind. On the contrary, I believe they were clearly designed for the profitability of the mutual fund company and their sales representatives. Here's why . . .

Let's pretend you and I serve on the board of directors at a very large, well-known mutual fund company. If our fund company is anything similar to most fund companies, we typically have a fair number of our funds that are performing horribly at any given time. During one of our board meetings, the CEO of the company stands up and asks, *"What are we going to do about our thirty or so mutual funds that act as nothing but a financial drag to our company because the fund manager's performance is so poor over time that no intelligent investor would consider putting money into them? These funds represent a significant number of our investment offerings to the public, and they continue to be business losers."*

Now, let's stop pretending for a minute and realize that our hypothetical CEO's questions and concerns are actually not hypothetical at all. This type of problem is very much a part of the reality at almost every mutual fund company on the planet. You see, the fact is that the overwhelming majority of a mutual fund company's revenue and profits are usually generated from only a small percentage of the total funds they have to offer. In fact, it is likely true that across the entire mutual fund industry, most of a fund

> **As is true with the overwhelming majority of fund companies across the industry, the bulk of their funds are subpar performers, and thus, investors are hesitant to place their money in them.**

company's offerings are poor revenue sources and are probably seen as poor business ventures by the company. As is true with the over-whelming majority of fund companies across the industry, the bulk of their funds are subpar performers, and thus, investors are hesitant to place their money in them. If the fund performance is poor for too long, the company starts taking a "business" loss from the operations of the poorly performing fund.

With that in mind, let's go back to our hypothetical board of direc-tors meeting and our agitated CEO. Let's also keep the math simple, imagining that our fund company has a total of twenty-five mutual funds—ranging from basic money markets, to international funds, to large, small, and midcap funds. If our fund company is like most, probably just a few of its funds perform well enough to attract any investor's money. Also, like many actual fund companies, our hypo-thetical fund company likely has another few funds that are "OK" performers and do well enough to generate a decent profit over time. In total, we might only have about five to seven total funds out of our twenty-five that are really worth anything to us as a business. What, then, are we to do about the 75 percent of our funds that are lousy performers and thereby worthless to us as a business?

The question from our fictitious CEO is basically: "How do we get the public to invest in our lousy funds so that our business can make money off of them?" In real life, the answer to that ever-perplexing question has always been to fire the current fund manager and re-place him or her with someone else who may potentially be able to improve the performance. Once the performance gets better, the pub-lic will take notice and begin sending their hard-earned money into the fund, and the fund company will eventually start turning a profit via the fees they charge the investors.

The problem, however, is that this approach has rarely (if ever) worked out. Fund companies seem to have a virtual revolving door when it comes to hiring and firing fund managers in the interest of improving performance. Just look at the management tenure of al-most any fund in the industry. Most funds are managed by someone (or a group of people) who has only been there a relatively short time versus the total time frame of the fund's existence. Why? Because the pressure for fund managers to perform is excessive, and the resulting turnover rate is fast and furious. There are simply far fewer great fund managers than there are funds to manage. So, what's a fund company to do when the public doesn't send their money because of poor performance? What can the fund company possibly do to turn an otherwise undesirable fund into a profitable business entity? The answer, in my opinion, came in the way of what is now known as "Target Date Funds."

Let's once again go back to our fictitious board of directors meeting. Now, let's pretend that the CEO is done defining the problem. Let's also assume that the same old suggestion of firing the fund managers and replacing them with new ones has already been debated to no agreement. Then, at the last moment, a voice from the back of the room speaks up: "Sir, if you don't mind, might I offer a suggestion?" (I'm thinking this was one of the summer interns who wasn't too experienced—but they let him speak anyway). He went on to say, "You see, sir, people are basically stupid. So, here's what we can do, and they'll never know better. Why don't we just bundle a collection of our funds together in baskets based on certain time frames? We'll put three or four of our really good funds at the top of the list; add some of our middle quality funds, and then back fill the remaining ten to fifteen funds with our lousy performers that no one wants. We'll call these bundled baskets, 'Target Date Funds' and market them as professionally managed portfolios designed to become more conservative over time. The investor simply picks a date that works for their plans, then starts sending their money in. We, as the 'investment professionals,' then allocate the investor's money among each of the ten or fifteen or twenty funds that we've put into the basket, making certain that a constant amount of money flows into our poorly performing funds. Ultimately, if we can sell enough of these Target Date Funds, we can virtually guarantee a never-ending flow of money even to our worst-performing funds." Our fictitious boardroom would certainly have gone dead quiet at the end of that presentation, until, of course, the board voted to fire the current CEO and replace him with the summer intern.

The point of this fictitious board of directors and CEO is this: Target Date Funds typically make for less-than-desirable investments versus other alternatives. They are marketed as the latest and greatest next thing in the evolution of investment products for individual investors; but, in fact, they likely weren't created with the investor in mind at all. They were, instead, likely created to control and ensure a continuous flow of money to otherwise poor-performing funds that the public would typically not put their money into.

Here is the "telltale sign" that these products weren't necessarily designed with the investor in mind: If you own a Target Date Fund, take a close look at how much of your total dollars are invested in any one fund within the basket. You will often find that some of the most prestigious mutual fund companies in the industry routinely allocate 1 percent of your total assets to a certain fund within the basket (I've seen as little as a half percent in some cases). Now, let me ask you a question: "What benefit exists to the investor to have 1 percent of their money invested in any one single fund within the basket?" Sure, the fund family will preach the doctrine of "diversification"; but is that what's *really* going on?

Think about it . . . If I were to put 1 percent of your money into anything and that investment were to double, what would be the "net" impact to you? The answer, of course, is "negligible."

Now, let's go in the other direction. What if I put 1 percent of your money into an investment, and it went completely to zero? What would be the "net" impact in this case? The answer: You wouldn't even notice it!

The point is . . . Placing 1 percent of your money in anything is mathematically a wasted allocation. If that 1 percent does really, really well, you're hardly going to notice it. If that 1 percent does horribly, you're still hardly going to notice it. Certainly, the "doctrine of diversification" can't apply. There's no positive outcome from a 1 percent allocation, and there's no added risk mitigation, either. So, why, then, would seemingly intelligent, professional, well-studied investment managers from some of the industry's most reputable and well-known fund companies put 1 percent of anyone's money into any one investment? It makes no sense, right?

Wrong.

If you look at it from the point of view of the fund company, it makes all the sense in the world. You see, it's not that they're just wasting "your" 1 percent, it's that they're adding your 1 percent to all the other tens of thousands of investors who own the same Target Date Fund you

> **Why would a financial advisor ever recommend that an investor use a Target Date Fund?**

do. Together, those tens of thousands of "1 percents" start to add up to "multipercent" profits for the fund companies.

A more pressing and disturbing question is: "Why would a financial advisor ever recommend that an investor use a Target Date Fund?" The answer, I believe, is twofold. First, in my opinion, the overwhelming majority of so-called financial advisors have never taken a very serious look at how these products work (largely because they probably don't understand portfolio development and allocation models and thereby don't really possess the necessary skill set to evaluate most investments appropriately). Second, if you have one of these products, and an "advisor" recommended it, you are most likely (almost certainly, in my opinion) dealing with and paying for nothing more than a salesperson and not a true financial advisor who understands real money management strategies. As with many of the recommendations promoted by investment "salespeople," Target Date Funds represent the "Easy Button" and typically demonstrate a lack of understanding in the interest of convenience.

The bottom line is this: If you have Target Date Funds that have been recommended to you by your advisor, it's probably time to get another advisor . . .

CHAPTER V

"I'VE RECOMMENDED THESE FUNDS FOR YEARS . . ."—RUN!

OCCASIONALLY, I HAVE the pleasure of being invited to industry "round table" events and workshops. During these events, I often take the opportunity to chat with many of my professional colleagues and counterparts from other firms. These individuals typically represent some of Wall Street's most respected firms with stellar reputations. Whenever possible, I will ask some of these other advisors what investments they use for their clients and how they determine them. Interestingly enough (but not all too surprising), I rarely meet an advisor who answers that ". . . it depends on how certain investments are performing with respect to my clients' needs." When I do occasionally get an answer like that, I know I'm speaking with a real professional, worthy of his or her client's trust.

Sadly, though, the all too common answer is that advisors simply recommend to their clients the same set of mutual funds from the same mutual fund company that they have been recommending for years. And "yes," most of them recommend Target Date Funds as well (see the previous chapter). Again, the proverbial "Easy Button" . . .

Now, while I have never had the pleasure of attending a client meeting with one of these fine financial salespeople, I can assume that part of their "sales pitch" goes something like this: "I've been recommending these funds for years. I know the fund company very well and recommend them to all my clients who express the same goals as you have." Well, jeez, that sounds pretty professional and well thought out, wouldn't you agree? How could there be a problem with that?

Here's how: In the case of all actively managed mutual funds, they are managed by people. These people are charged with the responsibility of making the decisions of which stocks or bonds are going to be owned by the fund. These people are under significant pressure to perform. It doesn't take a rocket scientist to figure out that there is one gigantic, unavoidable variable at work here—the "human element." You see, it is rare—in fact, darn near impossible—to have a managed fund that demonstrates, year after year, consistent, long-term performance that is better than all other funds of similar type. It goes without saying that fund performance changes over time and from fund to fund. Almost no single fund outperforms its peer group of similar fund types on a consistent, year-over-year basis. However, at any point in time, there are almost always some funds that are out-performing everyone else in their category. The difficultly is that the great performers and the poor performers are often changing place with one another over time. If that is the case, then why would you have your money in funds that aren't performing at the highest level versus their peer groups? And—before you answer the previous question—let me fire another one at you: Do you *really* care which fund company your money is in? Assuming that you have the freedom to choose from multiple, highly rated fund companies, does it matter to you if your advisor were to recommend "ABC" funds or "CBA" funds? The answer—I hope—is "no"!

There should be, in my opinion, only one concern and care that any investor and their advisor should have. It should be to have your money invested in the best possible investment choices available for what you are trying to achieve. Period!

Let's face it, when clients sit down with an advisor, they believe that the advisor is "watching over their money," which implies that the advisor proactively makes changes to the client's investments as warranted, and when investment choices once recommended no longer are performing as desired. If the advisor is not actively monitoring the investments and is not making changes when need be, then the client has to ask himself, "What am I paying this person for . . .?"

> Let's face it, when a client sits down with an advisor, they believe that the advisor is "watching over their money."

My assumption is that every client of every financial advisor believes without a doubt that the reason that they have enlisted the services of their advisor is because they expect that the advisor is watching over their investments. In addition, it is the belief that the advisor is using some criteria that is more complex and sophisticated than that which the client could come up with on their own.

If those assumptions are true, and if an advisor was truly "watching over" a client's investments, then it stands to reason that the fund choices being used today most likely aren't the same ones that were recommended a few years ago. In line with that is that the selected investments being used are most likely not going to be part of the portfolio a few years from now. Why? Because funds that may have been recommended today because of stellar performance vs. similar funds in the industry will likely not be the best performers a few years from now. Remember: Performance between funds seems to rotate over time. The best funds of today often become the mediocre funds of tomorrow. And poorly performing funds today often can become the stars a few years from now. As such, a true financial advisor must monitor specific fund performance vs. similar funds in the industry. When it is discovered that the performance of a previously recommended fund begins to wane, the fund should be "fired and replaced" with a different but similar fund that is performing at the highest level. If the advisor employed this process, then the advisor could never say, "I recommend these funds to all my clients. I've been using them for years and know the fund company very well." And if you do hear an advisor say such a thing: Run! It's a sure sign that the advisor does absolutely zero research and probably spends more time monitoring his or her golf score than they ever will your investments.

Take my own practice as an example. I have a multitiered screening process that we apply in order to identify specific fund choices and other types of investments that we recommend to our clients. However, if all I ever did was use this screening process for the initial allocation of a client's portfolio, I'd be failing my clients. The value that comes behind the relationship is that my team and I run each and every investment through a screening process throughout the year! That means that we consistently continue to monitor our clients' investments to ensure that they continue to adhere to our minimum levels of performance relative to other similar investments which we are also monitoring. If, during our screening process, we find that an investment no longer meets our minimum performance levels, we "fire-and-replace" that investment. Period!

My team and I do this because we believe that our clients expect us to manage and maintain their accounts. Since that is what they expect, that is what they get. More importantly, every time we make a change to our client's investment lineup, our clients see specific evidence and proof that we are actually doing something for them. My question for most investors who are using financial salesmen is: "What is the evidence that your advisor is actually doing something for you?" If the answer is that he or she sends you a nice monthly or quarterly newsletter with a recap of past market activity, that's not a very good answer. You are paying your advisor and his or her firm to "manage" your money. If you can't explain what consistent and continuous process they are applying on your behalf, then it is a pretty good indicator that you are dealing with a "salesperson" and not a true financial advisor worthy of the fees he or she is charging you.

Here is, in my opinion, a dose of reality. If you have an advisor who tells you that he or she uses consistent, independent criteria for identifying which funds to use, then it stands to reason that your investment lineup will go through changes from time to time. In my process that we apply to our client accounts, we usually make one to two fund changes per year. Sometimes, more; sometimes, less. But all changes are made based off of specific criteria and minimum performance standards. Basically, we set a challenge for the mutual funds managers that make it into our clients' accounts: Stay at the top of your game, and you get to stay in our clients' portfolios. Perform less than expected, and we'll fire you and replace you in a second—no questions asked.

Again, if we are doing our jobs for our clients, there is almost no way that the investment lineup being used today for any client will be the same in a few years. It is more likely that many of the originally selected mutual funds would have been "fired-and-replaced" by then.

So, I'll ask again, "What evidence do you have that your advisor is actually doing anything for you?" The answer is not always obvious. However, if your advisor isn't doing anything for you, the evidence is usually crystal clear—because there isn't any!

The bottom line is this: If you are contemplating hiring an advisor who proudly states that they have been using the same investment funds for years and that they know the fund company very well, think about finding another advisor. Similarly, if you are currently working with an advisor and you cannot remember the last time he or she recommended a change in your investment lineup, it is likely time to look for another advisor.

CHAPTER VI

WHERE'S THE SERVICE (IN GOOD TIMES AND IN BAD)

IN THE INTEREST of full disclosure, I must now offer you a warning: You have finally made your way to the single chapter which describes the entire purpose of this book. When you think about it, everything in this book really drives at the question: "What is it that my financial advisor is doing for me?" Unfortunately, as you are probably learning, the answer lies somewhere between "not much" and "nothing!"

The essence of this book is that financial advisors, and anyone else who attempts to claim a relatively equal title and/or role, are, by definition, part of an industry known as the "Financial Services Industry." This is an interesting name since it implies "service"—yet, all too often, it really means "sales."

A true financial advisor will clearly identify what it is that they do for their clients over time. They

> They will provide you with clear and measurable criteria by which you can see that they are actually performing their duties.

will provide you with clear and measurable criteria by which you can see that they are actually performing their duties. And, as mentioned in the previous chapter, if all they do is mail you a nice quarterly newsletter created by their marketing department and return your phone calls when you call them, that doesn't count as much service. What we need to be seeing from the advisor is intelligent, proactive engagement in the continuous management process of your accounts.

The irony of all ironies is that clients need true financial advice and guidance when investments and/or markets are not performing as desired. No time in recent history can highlight this need better than the economic events of a decade ago, when the markets and global economies went into their biggest nosedives since the Great Depression. The shame of many so-called financial advisors is seen when I meet with client after client of other financial advisors, and I often ask them how their advisor helped them through the disastrous years of 2008 and 2009. Usually, they answer by saying that they lost a lot of money. To which I then say, "OK, most people saw their account values drop during that time. But what did your advisor have to say when those events were happening? How did he or she 'advise' you during that time?" All too often, the answer was, "I really didn't ever hear from my advisor." Unbelievable!

As a financial advisor myself, during a time in our nation's history marked by tremendous financial difficulties and shattering investor confidence, it brought to mind one of the most powerful learning moments of my life. I was twenty years old and had decided to join the United States Marine Corps. Although many of my Marine experiences have had lasting effects on me, maybe none had had as great an impression on me as when I was leading a squad of Marines through the forest on a training exercise. During our maneuvers, I led my men directly into an awaiting ambush. My men and I were taken completely by surprise. The forest exploded with gunfire and smoke. My men and I moved to take cover in any possible direction, only to be met by more of the well entrenched "enemy." We were surrounded with no place to go. Thankfully, this was only a training exercise. Had it been the "real thing," it would have ended in a slaughter of my men—with me in charge!

Finally, the exercise came to an end. And with the forest blanketed in thick smoke and the ringing of gunfire and explosions still in the air, the Marine Staff Sergeant running the training exercise came toward me. As if out of a movie and completely on cue, the smoke before us seemed to part in perfect symmetry. This Staff Sergeant's chiseled face, fierce eyes, commanding presence, and booming voice were all directed straight at me. I will never forget what he said. Despite my complete failure in this exercise and despite me leading my men directly to their "hypothetical" deaths, this embodiment of the perfect Marine came toe-to-toe with me, thumped his finger on my chest, and said, "This was an ambush—a worst-case scenario for any Marine in the field. But as a leader, this should have been your greatest moment to shine! Instead of taking the enemy head-on, you and your men scattered in every possible direction. With no control, no discipline, and no game plan for this type of situation, you failed!" He then paused, stared me down, and slowly said some of the most powerful words I've ever heard that still affect me today. He said, "Never forget, leadership is easy to assume when things are going well; it is *proven* when things go wrong . . ." Wow.

We spent the next few hours right there in the same spot working on strategies and maneuvers designed to increase the odds of our survival in the event of future, real-life ambushes. It was great military training, but the lesson was one for my entire life! My takeaway from that ambush and the following lecture was that people need "real" leadership, guidance, and direction *mostly* when things go wrong, not when things are going right. It is during the toughest times that we often see that rare person "step up" and show the world why they should be followed. We know this to be true in any profession—not just for warrior Marines.

And it should have been true during the most devastating financial crisis in our country's history since the Great Depression. When, back in 2008, the world's financial markets were in turmoil, your financial advisor should have been showing you his or her absolute best. During that crisis, your advisor should have been providing extraordinary levels of communication, clear and understandable strategies designed to limit potential losses, and constant updates to changes in account values. The financial crisis of 2008 was,

> . . . people need "real" leadership, guidance, and direction *mostly* when things go wrong; not when things are going right.

indeed, the moment for great financial advisors to shine and show you their true value. Unfortunately, very few embraced the opportunity.

It is absolutely beyond me that advisors all throughout the industry nearly disappeared during one of the worst financial crises in our country's history. The truth is that when things go wrong in the markets and clients' accounts start to lose value, that is precisely when clients need advice the most. Yet, very few clients actually received any, leaving them to wonder what the word "advisor" really stands for in the title "Financial Advisor."

A question I often ask investors is: "What is it that serves as evidence that your financial advisor is actually doing anything for you?" In almost every case, I get not much more than a blank stare as an answer. In the best cases, the client pauses for quite some time before a feeble attempt to provide an answer likely designed more to make them feel as though they were getting something for their money than to tell the actual truth. No one wants to think they're getting nothing in return for the fees they are being charged. So, to save face, investors will sometimes say that they get nice newsletters and that their phone calls are returned promptly.

When I pose such questions to clients, it is often the first time that they begin to be fully honest with themselves and realize that they are actually paying for nothing. This is not to say that there aren't any truly wonderful financial advisors out there. In fact, there certainly are. My intention here is not to demonize the entire industry, but instead, to make you aware of the difference between the good and the bad.

Let me put this in simple terms. I have a brother-in-law who is in the construction business. Specifically, he and his wife own a rather large, very successful drywall company in the Washington, D.C., area. They specialize in large, commercial projects often requiring thousands of sheets of drywall, multiple crews of skilled finish men, and countless man-hours. In their market, they are considered one of the best. They do great work and generate millions of dollars in revenue.

So, what is it that makes his company so successful? Why has he been so consistently able to gain some of the best and highest-paying projects in the market his company serves? Well, the answer is probably a lot of reasons. But I would suspect that much of the driving force behind why so many general contractors seek his company's services and continue to pay his fees is because every single time his company performs a job, the evidence of what the contractor is paying for is obvious. It quite literally is hanging on the wall in front of them! General contractors can visibly see whether the dry wall has been set squarely, if the seams are tight, and if the finished work is smooth. In short, customers of my brother-in-law's company can see the evidence of what his company does and the value that they provide via the quality of their work. And, as a result, they continue to gain new business even while their competition tries to chip away at them by lowering their prices.

The fact is that no matter what the industry, no matter what the service, most people are comfortable paying fees—even relatively high fees—provided they have concrete, clear evidence of the value being gained for those fees. Isn't this true for you as well? Think about it. Very few of us have a problem paying our electric bill every month. Sure, we'd love it to be lower, but we don't have a philosophical problem with paying our electric bills because we know what we're getting for them. Every time we walk into a room and turn on the light switch, the television, the dishwasher, our computers, and so forth, we are reminded what value we are getting by paying our electric bill. And if you've ever had the "pleasure" of being without power for a day or two, you quickly realize that you'd rather live in a world with electric bills than one without. Why? Because you can see the value for the fee.

So, what about your financial advisor? Are the services he or she provides you obvious? Is there concrete, measurable evidence of work and effort conducted on your behalf? Do you have regular, meaningful, and proactive communication from your advisor? Do you get reviews of all things happening that impact your financial life—not just those that the advisor makes money from? Can you clearly point out the value of the fees and what you are getting for them? For most, the answer, unfortunately, is "no."

The wizardry of the financial services industry is that it has done a magical job at convincing all of its customers that there really isn't any evidence available! After all, financial advisors are retained for their knowledge and expertise. And how do you measure intellectual capital? You can't see someone's thoughts. You can't measure one's ideas, can you? Blah blah blah . . . That's all a bunch of garbage! The truth is that most financial advisors open accounts with clients . . . and then disappear. What's worse is that the client believes that the advisor is back in the office watching over their money. Sadly, the client has been fooled.

If you believe that you have a superior financial advisor simply because he or she returns your phone calls in a timely manner, I would suggest that you have set the bar rather low—and your advisor thanks you very much for doing so! Now, don't misconstrue my point here. Returning phone calls in a timely manner is actually important. But it is just one of the *many* things your financial advisor must be extraordinary at. My point is that if you truly have a wonderful financial advisor who is worth the fees you pay him or her, you will be able to clearly define and measure the value of their service by more than just a returned phone call once in a while. And if you were working with that same financial advisor during the world markets' meltdown of 2008 and into 2009, then you should be able to look back at that time to truly gauge the value of your advisor. If your recollection of that time was that your advisor "stepped-it-up" and showed true leadership, then you're probably working with a good one. If, on the other hand, you don't have that recollection, then you likely need to find a new one.

CHAPTER VII

WEALTHY ADVISORS DON'T ALWAYS MAKE WEALTHY CLIENTS

I WAS HAVING dinner with a client of mine one evening. Professionally, he is a medical doctor with a very successful practice and has been a client for many years. Personally, though, we enjoy each other's company and share a common interest in our love for cars. Neither of us cares too much about "brand loyalty," and we just both really appreciate well built, well designed cars of any make and model. We can spend hours talking about the latest designs in sports cars, SUVs, sedans, and even minivans—it doesn't matter to us; we're just both avid car guys. In the end, we like to talk about cars that when you step back and look at them, you just say to yourself, "Wow, what a wonderful and good-looking piece of machinery . . ." So, as you can imagine, when he and I aren't talking about financial planning and portfolio risk management, we are most likely talking cars.

Well, during one of our obligatory car talks, it came to my mind that he drives a fairly modest SUV (a very nice SUV, but certainly not the high-end types that he so much seems to appreciate). So, I asked him, "Why, if you seem to appreciate higher-end cars, and you can certainly afford one, don't you drive one?" Truthfully, I found it a bit perplexing that a man with such significant financial means and a love for such cars doesn't just go out and get one. His answer was fascinating.

He said it was his feeling that it wouldn't look good to have a high-end, rather expensive car parked in his reserved parking space in front of his office. He felt that many of his patients are concerned with the already high costs of health care and their deductibles. He thought that if he had a premium, imported car parked in his space, it would send the wrong message. In his opinion, some of his patients might walk by an expensive foreign car and think to themselves, "How much does this guy make off of my medical problems . . .?"

I thought about his reply for a minute and realized that his feelings and thoughtfulness toward his patients' perceptions were probably right on. His answer then forced a discussion about the "messages" that practitioners of all professions are sending their clients or patients. So, I asked him, "Well, what's that say about me, and the message I'm sending you, since I do indeed drive a foreign car that many might say is on the higher end?"

> His answer then forced a discussion about the "messages" that practitioners of all professions are sending their clients or patients.

Interestingly enough, he gave me quite the opposite response than what I was expecting. It was his opinion that clients of financial advisors actually want to see their financial advisors wearing nice clothes, living in nice homes in nice neighborhoods, and, yes, even driving nice cars. Not lavish or ostentatious but nice. In short, he said, that in his opinion, people who have financial resources want to feel that the person who they have entrusted those resources to has at least a similar financial status—or maybe even a bit more than the client's financial status. Clients want to know that the person they've hired to manage their portfolio has, in turn, their own portfolio that they are managing as well. The assumption, of course, being that the advisor had created his or her wealth through shrewd and prudent investing and is that much more "qualified" to manage the client's money—interesting viewpoint, to say the least.

But at some level, I do agree. I would think that most people who engage the services of a financial advisor would, all things being equal, prefer to work with someone of experience and who has been in the business for some time vs. working with a "rookie" right out of college. Why? Simply because of two things: First, you want your advisor to have industry experience. Second, you hope that your advisor has some degree of personal investment success, and that much of the advice and guidance that he or she is giving to their clients, they are also applying to their own situation (sort of the "walk-the-talk" idea). And, of course, how could a person just out of school really understand a client's needs if they have none of those same needs? Makes sense at some level, right?

Well, there is an inherent trap in this kind of thinking. You see, while it certainly makes sense that a client would want his or her financial advisor to have some degree of their own wealth, the assumption that they became that way by investing and managing their own money is very likely a figment of the client's imagination. The bottom-line truth is that for the overwhelming majority of financial advisors, the manner in which they created their wealth was simply the result of charging high fees and commissions to their clients. The cumulative effect of doing so for many years resulted in the advisor's own degree of wealth.

So, be careful of the wolf in fine clothing. When meeting in a financial advisor's office, do not make the mistake of being overly impressed (or even influenced) by the fancy desk, the corner office, the awards and plaques, the fine suits, and, yes, the fancy foreign car parked out front. These visuals can go a long way in shaping our assumptions of the advisor's skills and abilities in the field of financial planning or portfolio management. Yet, they most often are nothing more than the result of being a fine "salesperson" who happens to be in the financial services industry. Being a great "salesperson" and being a great "financial advisor" are not necessarily the same thing, so don't make the mistake of viewing them as such.

So, the questions that beg to be asked are: "How then does one determine if a financial advisor is worth listening to (let alone *paying for* . . .)? How can you tell where the advisor's wealth came from and thus make an assumption as to whether they understand financial planning, asset management, and portfolio management at the highest levels? How can a potential client determine whether the advisor made his or her wealth as an 'investor' with 'skin-in-the-game' experience or just as a good 'salesperson'?"

The good news is that there is, indeed, a way to get these answers and know definitely whether your financial advisor created his or her wealth by investing their own money (which could possibly make him or her worth listening to) or by "selling" investments (which could possibly make him or her worthy of walking away from). The answer is to ask for the evidence. After all, a competent financial advisor is certainly going to ask a lot of questions about your money. Why not ask a few about theirs?

Think about it: I, as a financial advisor, am a very nosy and intrusive person. Before I even meet with someone the first time, I send them a comprehensive questionnaire that requests very detailed information regarding all of the financial details of their life. I ask for tax returns, investment account statements, insurance policies, household expenses, wills, estate planning documents, and almost anything else that you can imagine—pretty personal stuff. And you know what? People routinely provide every bit of it. Many times, they even bring me more than I've requested. When you think about it, it's an incredible amount of trust and faith that people show me very early in our relationship. No matter how long I've been in this business and no matter how much longer I remain in it, I am truly humbled at the level of trust that individuals put on my shoulders. It's an amazing degree of responsibility that I gladly accept.

With that in mind, I would suggest to you that what is "fair" for a financial advisor to ask of you should be fair of you to ask of them in return. What I mean by that is if a financial advisor is going to ask you to divulge an incredible amount of personal financial data, shouldn't you be able to ask the financial advisor for the same information about them? Seems fair, doesn't it?

And that's why I stand ready to show any client or prospective client not only how my current investment dollars are invested, but maybe more importantly, how I created my wealth and where it came from in the first place.

In my case, I can demonstrate to anyone who asks that my money today is managed in a similar (and in some cases exactly the same) manner as the recommendations I am making to my clients. I routinely present personal statements of mine to clients and prospective clients to show them that I follow my own recommendations. I show to anyone who asks (and even to some who don't) my tax returns spanning the seven-year period when I generated millions of dollars as a professional trader and seat owner on the Philadelphia Stock Exchange.

> It's an amazing degree of responsibility that I gladly accept.

As I like to point out to prospective clients, I either really did create my personal wealth as a trader and investor, or I grossly overpaid my taxes for many years.

My question to you is: "Will your financial advisor really show you his or her financials?" And, if so, can he or she demonstrate to you that they created their wealth by "investing" and risking their own money or simply by getting rich off the commissions and fees they've been charging their clients over the years? Doesn't it make sense that you'd rather listen to, pay for, and follow the advice of someone who's "been-there-and-done-it" vs. someone who's just following the company line? I think so. I bet you probably do too.

I THOUGHT THEY ACTUALLY "MANAGED" MY MONEY

ALTHOUGH THIS IS not the last chapter of the book, it is sort of along the lines of "saving-the-best-for-last." It has to do with one of the great misconceptions that many investors have of their financial advisor, or if they have all their money directly with a single mutual fund company.

When I meet with potential clients for the first time, and since my team and I take a household, comprehensive approach toward helping people, they are asked to have the premeeting organizer and questionnaire completed. We also ask that they have all supporting documents and statements so that we can conduct a proper review and analysis of what they own.

As you can imagine, at some point in the first meeting, we begin to look through each account they own. What is most common is that people tend to have multiple accounts and typically with more than one investment firm or mutual fund company. Now, you must keep in mind that I've done this a time or two. My experience has led me to the fact that I often know the answers to many questions before I ask them. As a result, I get to ask some fairly loaded questions (and again,

I almost always know the answer before I ask the question . . .).

One such question I like to ask just prior to looking at a potential client's statements is: "So tell me, who do you have currently managing your money?" As you can imagine, the answers often range from local, small financial advisory firms, local banks, and all the way up to the largest, most recognized brokerage firms and mutual fund companies in the business.

The operative word in my question is "managing"! This is a critically important word. In fact, if you look back to the Latin origins of the word, it means "to act" or to demonstrate "activity." The problem, though, is that investors believe (in fact they have total faith) that if they've opened an account with a financial advisor from any firm, that that firm is actively "managing" the account. After all, isn't that ultimately why the client hires a financial firm? People want the feeling and assurance that while they are off doing whatever takes up their time during the day (work, kids, grandkids, vacations, etc.), someone is in the background watching over their money and making prudent recommendations, right? In its simplest form, isn't that the essence of why anyone hires a financial advisor or places their money directly with any investment firm?

Unfortunately, in most cases, that is *not* what is happening. In fact, all too often, nothing could be further from the truth! The fact is that in most instances, *no one* is managing *anything* on behalf of the client. Think about it. If someone is "managing" anything, it would imply that you would see some degree of activity. Things would be changing over time. By just looking at someone's account statements, you can see that what they owned some number of years ago is exactly what they own today, showing beyond the shadow of a doubt that no one is really "managing" the account for the client's benefit.

In most cases, when a person engages the services of a financial establishment, very little is done with the client's assets after the firm receives them. All too common in my industry is that accounts are created, a series of investments are recommended, the money moves into the recommended investments, and then the work is over. The client's money can—and likely will—sit unchecked and unmanaged for a long, long time.

This is, in my opinion, a colossal failure and sales job of many of my so-called financial services colleagues. In these days of highly volatile markets, investors are craving—*almost begging*—for prudent advice, guidance, and management of their assets and accounts. That's why they become clients in the first place! There is an undeniable assumption on the part of the investing public, that whichever investment firm they hire, they believe the company and its staff are actually managing the client's money—and they're not!

Of great shame is that there are large numbers of financial advisors and the firms they work for that knowingly prey on and leverage the idea that clients want someone to watch over their money. They are quick to market themselves with words like "strength," "stability," and, of course, "trust." The implications in the marketing pitch are that clients can have faith and take comfort in the company's name and "trust" them to do the right thing on behalf of the clients.

So, let's ask the question, "What is it that the investing public is supposed to be trusting these firms to do?" The answer, I believe, is that people are trusting that the firm is watching over the client's money and keeping them protected when things go wrong. But is that what is actually happening? Sadly, in most cases, the answer is "no."

The good news is that it's pretty simple to identify a firm that isn't living up to its trust image. One way to do so is to look at your account statements over time. If you have had roughly the same exact holdings in your account since the day you opened it, I've got news for you: No one's managing anything for you! Think about it: On a global basis, the financial and economic landscape has changed in dramatic

> People are trusting that the firm is watching over the client's money and keeping them protected when things go wrong. But is that what is actually happening? Sadly, in most cases, the answer is "no."

and materially significant ways since the early 2000s. If the firm that you have your money with has not suggested or made significant changes in your accounts since then, it might be time to ask them what it is you're paying them to do. I would also suggest this to be true for shorter time frames as well. This is because if you were convinced to allocate some of your money to a certain investment, say, three years ago, because it was "the best choice in its respective peer group," the odds of that still being true a few years later are not very high. So, investments need to be monitored and changed over time. If you see no evidence of this on your statements from one year to the next, then your assumption that the firm you have your money with is actually "managing" your money is probably not so accurate.

The bottom line is this: If you are holding accounts with a firm or an advisor, and you believe that their role is to "manage" and "watch over" your money, there's a real simple way to test that belief. Simply look for the evidence. If they routinely make proactive changes to your accounts (which means they suggest and/or make changes without you having to suggest it first), then you are likely getting pretty good help and have someone worth paying. If, however—like most people I meet—changes or recommendations are not being made, then you likely got "sold," and it's time to fire them and go find some real help.

PAY-TO-PLAY

I BELIEVE THAT every investor who sits down with a financial advisor does so for the following two reasons: First, they want someone to help them grow their wealth in ways that the investor doesn't already know. Second, they want the advisor to do it in a way that doesn't expose them to unnecessary and unknown risks. No matter how old or how young someone may be, no matter how wealthy they are or aren't, no matter what their stage in life, all investors want those two basic things from their financial advisor.

How an advisor delivers on those two items can vary from client to client. Some clients are still quite young and are in the accumulation of wealth phase. Other clients may have already retired and what is of most importance to them is the preservation of their wealth in order to be able to live off of it or to pass on an estate to their children or charities. Strategies and applications may change and be different from client to client based on their specific needs, but the idea of growing wealth and protecting wealth from risk exposure that the client may not be aware of are universal across all clients.

But what, on the other hand, is it that most financial advisors want? Is it to actually deliver beyond their client's expectations? Probably not. Unfortunately, most financial advisors are interested in just one simple goal: How to generate maximum commissions and fees with minimum effort.

This, of course, creates a natural conflict of interest and disconnect between the needs of the client and the desires of the advisor. The only question that remains then is this: "How do you know if the advisor you're working with is the type that only cares about you as far as his or her ability to charge you commissions and fees, or, if your advisor really has your best interests at heart and truly wants to show you how to create and preserve your wealth more efficiently?" The answer, I believe, is in three words: *comprehensive financial planning*.

You see, most financial advisors are only interested in growing their business via charging their clients as many fees and commissions as possible. This is why most financial advisors try not to spend very much time talking to people who don't have some "minimum" amount of investable money. It is also why they don't spend much

> **You see, most financial advisors are only interested in growing their business via charging their clients as many fees and commissions as possible.**

time talking to prospective and current clients about financial items that they can't charge any fee on (like Social Security and pension strategies, for example).

Let me explain it this way: Experience has taught me that most people's wealth is concentrated in two areas: first, their home, and second, their employer's retirement account (like a 401(k), 403(b), 457, or TSP). Think about it . . . Most people only a few years away from retirement have likely lived in their current home for quite some time. And while real estate values are still not quite as high as they once were, most "soon-to-be" retirees have been in their current homes long enough that they have likely experienced some amount of price appreciation and have paid down their mortgage enough so that they have a large degree of built-up equity in their home.

The other great source of wealth for most "soon-to-be" retirees is their employer-sponsored retirement account(s). Often, people have been contributing to their 401(k) (or another type of employer-sponsored account) for decades. As a result, there are significant values in these accounts. For many, there may be hundreds of thousands—and even millions of dollars—in these accounts.

Now, let's just say that you're a typical fifty-six-year-old. You've owned your current home for almost fifteen years and have roughly $300,000 in appreciated equity. You've also been with the same employer for the last eighteen years and have been diligently contributing to your 401(k) for that entire time. In fact, your 401(k) now represents the single largest pool of money you have. And, naturally, that makes your 401(k) the most important component of your investment and retirement savings plan.

Let's also assume that you're married and that both you and your spouse have managed to save other monies in other accounts. For example, you may have a Rollover IRA from a previous employer or maybe a Roth and a few mutual fund accounts as well. But if you're like most people, the total value of your other accounts all added together is still dwarfed by the total wealth you have created in your home and your employer's 401(k) account.

Now comes the all-too-familiar scenario: Let's say you and your spouse now decide it's time to speak with a financial advisor. How would you know if the advisor you choose to meet with is actually interested in helping you or helping him or herself? Easy. Just pay attention to what they focus the most on and the types of questions and information they ask of you.

You see, when presented with the above described hypothetical prospect, the overwhelming majority of financial advisors will likely spend considerable amounts of time and effort on how they can "manage" the other accounts (the Rollover IRA, the Roth, etc.). However, you will often notice that they simply glide over any credible suggestions and will spend materially less time strategizing how to manage your 401(k) and/or your home equity the best way possible. Yet, these are the very components most people need the most guidance on; they're the largest components of most people's wealth! For most people, their home equity and employer-sponsored retirement accounts are the part of their financial picture that they actually want the most guidance on since it will likely be those parts that they will need to live off of. Yet, most financial advisors will likely just discuss them in passing as they go about describing how much they can do for you on your other accounts. Why is this? Simple. Most financial salespeople couldn't care less where you actually need the most help. They care most about what accounts they can charge fees on—and as a result, *those* are the items they focus their discussions on.

This, of course, falls under the umbrella of the time-tested phrase, "actions speak louder than words." But be careful here . . . Many of the best financial salesmen have learned their craft well. It is not enough that the advisor simply asks you about your employer-sponsored retirement account; it is not enough that they ask you to provide your home equity estimate on their financial questionnaire. It is that when they present a plan to you, the employer-sponsored account and your home equity are fully incorporated within the strategy of that plan. In fact, it stands to reason that if your employer-sponsored retirement account and home equity are the largest components of your wealth, then these two items should obviously be the "cornerstones" of a well thought out and strategically sound retirement plan. Remember, "actions," not "words." The wolf in sheep's clothing is the crafty financial salesperson who "asks" about home equity and employer-sponsored retirement plans during your initial meeting, but then when he or she gets back to you with a plan, those two items are conspicuously downplayed almost to the point of being rendered irrelevant. That's, of course, a classic "bait-and-switch" tactic that we've all fallen for a time or two in our lives. Don't let it happen this time. The consequence could be life-altering.

So then, what should you be on the lookout for? How does someone interviewing financial advisors know whether that person has their household's best interests at heart before they decide to divulge all of their personal information to someone? Here's how: When interviewing a financial advisor, ask to see an example of a typical financial plan they have presented to someone with similar financial characteristics as you. If they say they can't produce one for "privacy reasons" (or any other reason), simply smile and bid them farewell. The reality is, they can indeed show you an example of a real financial plan that is cleared of any personal client data. In reality, a true professional will likely have one available prior to you even asking.

If the advisor does provide an example, look at it carefully. In most cases, it's not really a "plan"; it's more just a "crunching of the numbers" and a financial "projection." Most of what is presented as a "plan" is really just a bunch of colorful charts and graphs designed to impress the potential client; however, it is actually void of any real substantive guidance and suggestions. If this is the case, then simply smile and bid that advisor a fond farewell too.

But if, as will be the case if you keep looking for the right advisor, they produce an example of a recent plan that clearly highlights a client's employer-sponsored account and suggestions on how to maximize the plan more efficiently; and if the plan also shows how the client's home equity fits into their greater financial picture, then sit back and relax. You are likely sitting face-to-face with a very rare breed of financial advisor whose interests are the well-being of their clients.

Now, a point of clarity before I close this chapter out. I am not implying that the kind of financial advisor you should be looking for is not at all interested in the growth of his or her business. To the contrary. There is nothing wrong at all with a competent, well-meaning, client-focused financial advisor who also happens to make a good living practicing his or her craft. After all, they do run a business, and any person in business, naturally, wants to see it grow. But please appreciate that there is a materially significant difference between the financial salesperson who's daily focus is just to find new prospects to sell their financial wares to and the truly wonderful financial advisor who understands that his or her business is likely to grow beyond their wildest dreams if they just adhere to the concept of helping their clients first. A great financial advisor and one worthy of your attention and money is usually someone who is goal-oriented him- or herself. But they know beyond a shadow of a doubt that the only true way to achieving their specific goals is to help their clients achieve theirs first.

Great advisors are who you are looking for. They are worth every penny of what they charge their cli-

> Great advisors are who you are looking for. They are worth every penny of what they charge their clients.

ents. The proof, of which, is embedded within the strategic plans they create for their clients. Just ask to see one, and you'll quickly separate the superstars from the mere salesmen.

DISCIPLINE AND STRATEGY, NOT JUST SOMEONE'S OPINION

HAVE YOU EVER had to see a doctor for something more than just a bump or a bruise? Have you ever had the pleasure of seeking a doctor's "opinion" on something that might possibly be life-threatening? If so, did you ever also seek out a "second opinion" from another doctor? I have. And if you haven't, just give life some time, and you probably will one day.

For me, it was a simple and routine visit to my dermatologist. Both my parents and my wife had been after me for quite some time to get a full dermatological evaluation. I delayed acting on their advice for as long as I could. But finally, at age thirty-nine, I figured I'd better go for no other reason than to quiet them down. And so, I went.

Now, it is important to appreciate that I am of Irish ancestry—*very* Irish ancestry, to be exact! That means that there's a bit of a red tinge to my otherwise brown hair, a face full of freckles, and a very fair skin tone . . . Which all adds up to one thing: When I'm out in the sun, I burn (badly and quickly)!

It's also important to know that as a kid, I grew up before the appreciation of good SPF sunscreen. In fact, as a teenager in the '70s and

'80s, I never really concerned myself with what getting sunburned every other week would mean over time. Heck, I can remember lying out in the sun and actually applying baby oil to my face and arms in some distorted attempt toward obtaining the "savage tan." And "savage" it was. So much so that I was achieving irreparable damage to my body—damage where the true impact would not surface until many years later.

So, there I was, no longer the careless, ignorant kid in the sun, but now a grown man in my doctor's office. The exam I had been putting off for so long was quick and easy. When done, the good doctor said the following to me, "I have some good news and some bad news." He, naturally, gave me the choice of deciding which I wanted first. I decided to go with the bad news first so I could at least end the appointment on a high note. He told me that I most certainly will have skin cancer one day. He said the ignorance of my youth had finally begun to show itself and that hidden damage I'd caused my skin was starting to appear. Indeed, there was already at least one spot on me that the doctor had expressed great concern about.

"Well, if that's the bad news, what's the good news?" To which he said that I shouldn't concern myself one bit about my "someday" skin cancer. He said that as long as he has now been made aware of the potential situation, he should be able to spot any problem areas and deal with them before they become anything too serious. In other words, he was professionally aware of the potential risks but was competent and experienced enough to prescribe and implement specific risk management strategies that would, if monitored consistently, reduce my risk to nothing more than an occasional and uncomfortable annoyance. I couldn't help but think to myself, *What a wonderful portfolio manager this guy would have made . . .*

Now, the purpose of this little story is not to get everyone who grew up in the "pre-SPF" era to run out and get a full dermatological body exam (although that wouldn't be such a bad idea), but instead, to call attention to the difference between the implementation of a specific strategy based on the result of imperial data, and that which is based on a salesman's opinion.

My dermatologist prescribed for me a management protocol only after having gone through some scientific methodology to determine what my issues either were or weren't. He then rendered his opinion of what I have and how to treat it.

The word "opinion" is an interesting one. The fact is that a doctor who is truly at the top of his or her game is never giving an off-the-cuff "opinion." The most competent of doctors are in the business of rendering a specific treatment protocol based on science, research, and mountains of historical data that combine to strongly suggest specific appropriate responses to whatever the ailment or injury the patient has. In a very real way, I am not interested in a doctor's off-the-cuff opinion. I do, however, care very much about his application and understanding of the science of medicine.

But what is it about someone's opinion when it comes to investing? It seems that so many investors are so quick to pull the trigger on an investment just because they heard someone's opinion on television. I have seen investors and even professional traders get so caught up in the opinions of a slick-talking, overly confident financial services sales pitch that they moved hundreds of thousands of dollars in the direction of the advisor's opinions.

Now, let's cut to the chase. I am very clearly saying that financial advisors' *opinions* are irrelevant! I'm telling you to stop investing and risking your household's hard-earned dollars based on someone's "opinion." Now, that's a pretty incredible statement given that I make my living largely by advising clients

> I'm telling you to stop investing and risking your household's hard-earned dollars based on someone's "opinion."

what to do with their money. It's also a rather interesting statement in that hardly a week goes by that a client or prospect doesn't ask me for my opinion on something.

But in reality, I try to offer my clients as little of my "opinion" as possible. I feel that too many investors simply follow their advisor's advice blindly. Interestingly enough, if ever you were going to find an advisor that you were going to follow blindly, I think that with my background and experience as a former Wall Street brokerage firm employee-turned-stock exchange floor trader, that my opinions would be worthy of following blindly. Yet, with all that background and experience, my clients have heard me say over and over that I won't let them follow me blindly.

Instead of offering my opinions, I offer my clients specific, clear strategies designed to provide the greatest opportunity for them to achieve their financial goals that are based solely on academic studies of markets, volatility, diversification, portfolio management, and other measurable data that impact investment strategies.

If you turn on any financial news show, you won't wait more than ten minutes before you hear some so-called financial professional spout off about the important reasons you should have your money invested in his idea. Then wait another ten minutes to hear yet another so-called financial professional tell you why the first person is wrong and that what you should *really* do is follow some different opinion. The same is true in the print media as well. It is all too common to read one financial magazine one month that is promoting a certain investment idea, and then two months later, read a competing magazine that suggests just the opposite. This, certainly, makes absolutely no sense. However, if you can get to the point where you can recognize that there are just relentless opinions coming at you one after another, then there's really no harm in them. The problem is that most people believe that these relentless opinions are actually sound investment advice. Worse yet, they actually follow them!

So then, the obvious question is: "Who should you listen to?" Even more, "How do you decipher sound investment advice from a worthless opinion?" The answers can be found in the financial advisor's processes. You should only be dealing with an advisor who clearly lays out nonbiased, systematic, and disciplined approaches for choosing any recommendations he or she makes, from stocks to insurance products; from mutual funds and ETFs to annuities and everything else in between. If the financial advisor you're dealing with doesn't have a multilevel screening process of specific criteria by which they identify what to recommend as being best for each client's needs, you are very likely dealing with a salesperson who is skilled only at speaking their worthless opinion with such confidence that people actually take action based on it.

Process. Process. Process. Ask your advisor to clearly explain the steps taken to identify the quality and prudence of one mutual fund over all the others that could potentially be recommended; one stock vs. another; one life insurance policy vs. another; one annuity vs. another; or one "whatever they're recommending" vs. another. If their explanation isn't robust, multifaceted, and in-depth, I'd suggest you smile and walk away. It is very likely that the only reason they are "recommending" any specific investment or product to you is that they have no real clue about what they are doing and are just spouting off the same half-baked, noncredible opinion to you as they did for the person they met with prior to meeting with you.

If you are seriously considering hiring a financial advisor and following his or her recommendations as "trusted" advice and guidance, I'd suggest you make certain that most of their recommended strategies and products be based on and rooted in the sound application of investment and financial management theory and academic study. They should take time to educate you on their methodology. You should be impressed by its thoroughness, discipline, and lack of emotion or opinion. If you're not, just leave. Don't bet your future and everything you've accumulated on someone's "opinion." You're worth more than that!

CHAPTER XI

BLAME IT ON THE MARKETS

AS HAS BEEN referenced in earlier chapters of this book, the economic and investment environment during this writing is particularly volatile and fragile. Many investors are still sitting on the sidelines from the carnage of 2008 and are still holding onto losses and fears.

Hardly a week goes by that when I meet with a prospective client, he or she is quick to point out some of their accounts which have posted losses of 20, 30, or even 40 percent or more at one time or another. I, of course, let them tell me their stories of how they came to have the specific investments that ultimately caused such a loss. All too often, and no matter who the person, I hear the same stories over and over: Stories of how they listened to a friend who seemed to know a lot about investments and followed his advice until it ultimately resulted in failure; or, they listened to the sage advice of their brother-in-law or other family member who does their taxes; or, they picked the investments themselves after researching them online; and, naturally, they read lots of financial articles and even used to subscribe to financial newsletters.

It is usually at that point that I ask my favorite follow-up question . . . a question to which I already know the answer. I ask, "So, what is it that this friend of yours, or tax preparer, or financial newsletter has to say when you ask them why you lost 40 percent on your investments after following their advice?" The answer always is something along the lines of, "Well, they tell me it was unavoidable because the whole world was suffering losses; everything went down. What could be done . . .?"

What a pathetic answer! What a tremendously disgusting display of passing the buck and taking no blame. Worse, though, is that investors and clients alike actually accept it as a reasonable and very rational "fact of life."

Mutual fund companies, brokers, financial advisors, and almost anyone involved in the financial services industry are all too quick to blame the markets for any financial loss and then take all the credit for positive outcomes. If you have heard this type of thing from your advisor or investment firm, I'd say you deserve more—and you should start *demanding* it! You need to get to the point where you understand that the "blame-it-on-the-market" response is a clear indicator that the individual or firm that you are dealing with has no greater skill at investment management than you have. In fact, by their very own admission, they are clearly telling you that their only approach for your money is to put it into some investment and then just sit back and wait to see what happens.

Think about it . . . There are likely many reasons why someone would have a financial advisor. But wouldn't you think that one of the primary motivators that drives people to seek one out is the belief that the advisor knows more; understands more; and is simply "smarter" than the client when it comes to investments and overall financial plan-

> Sadly though, most financial advisors are nothing more than salespeople who likely don't know much more about investing than does the client.

ning matters? Sadly, though, most financial advisors are nothing more than salespeople who likely don't know much more about investing than does the client. And, in reality, it may even be the case that the client actually knows more than the financial advisor because while the client at least reads a few financial articles from time to time, the financial salesman spends more of his or her time reading "how-to-sell" articles!

It stands to reason that if someone receives compensation for recommending and managing investments for you, that they ought to have some measurable skill set at being better managers of your money than you would be. And I'm certain you would agree that their specific skill set should be most noticeable (and most valued) when investment environments are at their worst.

Look at it this way . . . If you could look into a crystal ball and see that the stock market was going to go up 20 percent each and every year for the next thirty years, would you actually need a financial advisor? Of course not! You'd simply put all your money in an S&P 500 Index fund and sit back and get rich. But, in reality, you don't really hire a financial advisor just to help you get rich. What you really need them for is to make certain that you don't suddenly get poor when things go wrong. And investments, economies, and markets do, indeed, go wrong from time to time. In fact, during the years that I was a stock exchange floor trader, one of the nation's leading financial news organizations used to play an annual game. For a few consecutive years, on the first business day of each year, they would actually get a monkey to throw a handful of darts at a printed listing of stocks that they taped to the wall. This was during the mid- to late '90s while Wall Street was roaring to record highs year after year due to the surge of the "dot.com" era. And, wouldn't you know it, as a very open and highly critical impression of mutual fund managers, the dart-throwing monkey almost always outperformed the vast majority of fund managers by year-end, highlighting beyond the shadow of a doubt that when things are going well in the economy and investments seem to move higher, most investors don't need any help at all to do well. Indeed, they could just as easily rely on a monkey!

But the question that begs to be asked is: "Did the dart-throwing monkey ever start performing poorly against the mutual fund industry?" And the answer is absolutely "yes." You see, that very same financial news organization who exuberantly delighted at seeing the monkey beat the majority of fund managers and who openly began suggesting that people could do better on their own, no longer does their fun little annual game. Why not? Because what they learned was that the stock market and economies don't always just go up. In fact, beginning around 1999 and through most of the early 2000s, the surge of the dot.com era came to a painful and dramatic end. The environment changed, and a new era of volatility and loss took over. And the monkey suffered losses so great versus those of the professional managers that the monkey actually lost almost every gain it made in the previous years, clearly demonstrating that in years of market turmoil, a skill set greater than just the ability to throw darts is required!

So, what about *your* advisor? Does he or she show you a measurable skill set at helping to protect your household's net worth when things are not going as planned? If they do, then you've got a good one. If they don't, it's time to question what you're paying for.

Finally, keep this in mind: Certain universal truths are just as applicable in our everyday lives as they are to the management of money. Isn't it mostly true that we see the strength and value of others, not when times are going well, but, most often, when things are at their worst? Of course, so. The same holds true for a competent financial advisor whose services are worth paying for. Truth be told, you likely won't feel that you need a financial advisor when economies and markets are showing year-over-year gains. But you *will* see the value in having that advisor when things go poorly.

Proper, appropriate, and well diversified planning should have—at its core—strategies designed and specifically in place to help keep your entire household portfolio somewhat insulated from catastrophic losses due to major market sell-offs.

So, if the markets suffer through significant losses and your account or portfolio suffers essentially the same degree of losses, then you're probably not dealing with the right financial advisor. If the only thing your advisor can say when you question poor results is something like: ". . . well, that's part of investing . . ." then you're likely dealing more with a sales rep than with a competent advisor who's really worth paying for. Fire that person and seek out another.

CHAPTER **XII**

IT CAN BE DONE BETTER

OKAY, I KNOW what you're thinking: You feel as though you've just spent a large chunk of your valuable time reading nothing but negativity, but that's not really the point. What I've tried to do throughout these pages is awaken and enlighten you to the fact that maybe, just maybe, your so-called financial advisor, as nice and as enjoyable you may feel he or she is, might not be the competent professional that you believe that person to be. You might also be thinking that over the years, you've actually been spending quite a considerable amount of your hard-earned money doing not much more than lining the pockets of someone else who really wasn't much more versed on competent, intelligent financial planning and investment strategies than you are.

But don't be upset. It wasn't your fault. You were duped by an industry that has created a mastery at selling its empty services even to the smartest and shrewdest of us all . . . An industry that intentionally confused its clients with clever terminologies and products.

It is at this juncture that I must interject a point of clarity. As stated in the Preface of this book, it is with the investor in mind. Period! But do not misconstrue that as being an attempt to discredit the financial services industry. Nothing could actually be further from the truth. My objective in writing this book is not to put financial advisors out of business, but instead, to usher in a new era of well-educated clients who demand more of them. Let's face it, financial advisors, regardless of their level of competency, are people who can and do make significant incomes for themselves and their families. The average financial advisor who has been in business ten years or more can easily be making a six-figure income. One can even argue that given the relative education needed for someone to claim the professional title of "Financial Advisor," versus the educational demands toward becoming an attorney or medical doctor, financial advisors may be some of the most generously compensated professionals in our society. With that in mind, is there anything wrong with demanding extreme levels of competency from them? Wouldn't you demand such competency from a medical doctor about to perform surgery on you or a loved one? What about from an attorney that you may engage to help defend you or your business from a frivolous lawsuit? Would you demand excellence from them given the level of compensation they would be receiving? Certainly, you would. And you should!

Hey, there is nothing in the world wrong with paying someone a fee. Maybe even nothing wrong with paying someone a relatively high fee . . . as long as they are worth it. And a great, competent financial advisor is indeed worth it to many. The problem is that too many sales-

> **And a great, competent financial advisor is indeed worth it to many.**

men are actively confusing people into believing that they are that competent advisor—when, in fact, they aren't even close.

Let's do the math. A typical fee-based financial advisor managing $100,000 for a client might charge 1.5 percent of the assets per year. That would be a dollar amount of $1,500. Assuming some growth in the account value over time, the client might end up paying the advisor $20,000 over ten years. That's 20 percent of the initial investment. That's a lot of money!

Let's say you have three times that amount with your advisor; you might be forking over as much as $60,000 over the next ten years. Have a million with an advisor, and you could be spending more than $200,000 over the next decade. Add to that the fact that most people who enter into a relationship with a financial advisor tend to stay with that advisor for the rest of their lives, so you're talking about significant sums of money going to your advisor.

Therefore, it really comes down to two questions: 1. Is your financial advisor worth it (and a really good one is)? 2. Is it too much for you to demand that the advisor you're working with be of extreme competence given the amount of money you'll be paying that person over time? For most, the answer is likely "no" for both questions.

So then, what to do? Where does one go to find this elusive and rare financial advisor who's actually worth following? Who's worth believing in? Who's worth paying? Well, unfortunately, there's no easy answer. However, now that you are armed with the information covered in this book, you are now prepared to interview a number of potential financial advisors. You will likely find many "salesmen" before finding the one that's right for you, but that's okay. Don't be mean to them. They're likely very nice people, just lousy advisors. When you've discovered that they're nothing more than a "salesperson," simply smile and tell them you need to be getting on your way.

But then, it *will* happen! The "eureka!" moment. You'll find that one—the one who is prepared to show you his or her accounts and prove to you that they believe so much in what they are doing that they even invest and risk their own financial future in some of the very same strategies and ideas that they recommend to their clients.

You'll know you've found your new financial advisor when he or she explains that they generate very little, if any, of their income from charging commissions and transaction fees to their clients. Instead, they will happily show you the annualized fee schedule with reduced fee "breakpoints" for higher asset levels.

You'll know you've found the right financial advisor when they spend significant time learning about you and your household's current financial situation and future goals and lifestyle aspirations before they ever render a single suggestion or recommendation.

You'll know you've found a financial advisor worth paying for when the cornerstone of his or her overall financial plan for your household is focused on what strategies are in place if things don't go as planned. A competent financial advisor should spend quite some time articulating what strategies are in place to help insulate your household from suffering disastrous losses in the event markets sell-off dramatically. Remember, risk management is really what you're hiring someone to do.

And, finally, you'll know if you've found your new financial advisor if he or she emphasizes that he or she must maintain an open and consistent line of communication with their clients.

The right financial advisor, worthy of your time, belief, faith, and money, may or may not come from a large national firm. He or she may or may not have the same background or experiences that I have. But one thing will be sure . . . When you find a financial advisor that isn't likely to fail you—and they are indeed out there—sit back and relax; you're in good hands.

> **But one thing will be sure: When you find a financial advisor that isn't likely to fail you—and they are indeed out there—sit back and relax; you're in good hands.**

CPSIA information can be obtained
at www.ICGtesting.com
Printed in the USA
BVHW081550050821
613735BV00012B/1167